The Light of the "I"

GEORG KÜHLEWIND

# The Light of the "I"

## Guidelines for Meditation

EDITED AND INTRODUCED BY

Christopher Bamford

LINDISFARNE BOOKS
2008

Originally written in English by Georg Kühlewind, *The Light of the "I"* was translated into German by Evelies Schmidt and published as *Licht und Freiheit: Ein Leitfaden fur die Meditation* by Verlag Freies Geistesleben, Stuttgart, Germany, 2004.

The present edition is an edited version of the original English. It is published with the kind permission of Verlag Freies Geistesleben.

Published by Lindisfarne Books
610 Main Street, Great Barrington, Massachusetts 01230
www.lindisfarne.org

Library of Congress Cataloging-in-Publication data

The light of the I : guidelines for meditation / edited and introduced by Christopher Bamford ; Georg Kühlewind.
    p. cm.
 ISBN 978-1-58420-059-8
 1. Attention. 2. Meditation.  I. Bamford, Christopher, 1943- II. Kühlewind, Georg.
 BF321.L54 2008
 158.1'2--dc22
                        2008018879

Printed in the United States

# CONTENTS

# INTRODUCTION

*by Christopher Bamford*

BORN GYÖRGY SZEKELEY IN 1924 IN BUDAPEST, Hungary, Georg Kühlewind was a meditation teacher, philosopher, and writer, who assumed the *nom-de-plume* of "Kühlewind" or "Cool Wind" (a name taken from one used in youthful role-playing games) during the Communist years when, for obvious reasons, it was necessary to be discrete if one wished to write about spiritual matters.

The son of a doctor, he was artistically and intellectually gifted. From his earliest years, he played the piano, later even contemplating a career as a concert pianist; at the same time, he was deeply and precociously fascinated by questions of consciousness. Both of these—a love of music and a love of consciousness—would accompany him for the rest of his life.

At fifteen, his interests lay in Freudian psychoanalysis, Jung, and the history of religion and culture. By seventeen, he was a student of Karl Kerenyi, later Jung's collaborator and friend, celebrated for his spiritual and psychological commentaries on the Greek Mysteries and the Greek gods. Kerenyi inspired him to learn Latin and Greek and to consider becoming a classical philologist.

Topping off this heady mix, by eighteen, he had also already encountered Rudolf Steiner's Anthroposophy and read deeply in it. Clearly, he was already on a spiritual path. He had begun a program of seeking to "erase" from himself "all habits, traditions, and conventionality."

What would have happened next if the Second World War, which until then had spared Hungary and Budapest its worst excesses, had not then reached its cruel, inhuman, perhaps inevitable conclusion, we do not know. But it did. And Kühlewind returned from his concentration camp experience inwardly a "desert." Nothing could ever be exactly as it was before. Therefore, when it came time to chose what he would study, he chose with complete freedom something to which he had no prior relationship: physical chemistry.

Thus, professionally, he became a physical chemist, teaching in a technical university for over thirty years and doing important research in the fields of absorption, catalytic processes, surface chemistry, and chemical engineering. He was very successful, patenting many inventions and enjoying research fellowships all over the world from Germany and Italy to China.

But science was only his outer path. Inwardly, after the war, he continued to read extensively, even prodigiously, in Anthroposophy. He became an "expert" in it. Then, one day, he experienced a shocking revelation. Suddenly, everything he thought he knew seemed sterile and unproductive, even meaningless. He had amassed vast amounts of spiritual "information," but where it really counted—on the inner path, the path of spiritual practice, which should have made what he "knew" a living reality—he had achieved nothing. "At this point," he writes:

I nearly threw out the whole of Anthroposophy. Then I had a significant dream. I remembered one of Steiner's books, *The Philosophy of Freedom*, which I knew I had not understood. I began to study this book and all Steiner's other epistemological works. I wanted to give them a "last chance." Rigorously, without looking into the more esoteric works, I wanted to understand the epistemological works by themselves alone. After about half-a-year, I knew the direction I had to take. I saw the errors I had made and the misunderstandings (felt as understandings) I had committed. I had understood that the level of real understanding is not the level used in other sciences but is, minimally, the level of living, experienced thinking, i.e., the process, not the thought. From this moment on (about 1958) I slowly began on the path of inner schooling....

Neither Kuhlewind's dissatisfaction nor his subsequent realization is surprising. Steiner's so-called epistemological works are extraordinarily difficult to grasp. While appearing to be works of philosophy, they are in fact more like manuals of inner work; or at least a report or personal account of inner work. In this sense, Steiner's epistemological works form the foundation for all of his anthroposophical spiritual research: they establish its principles or method. This is especially true of *The Philosophy of Freedom*, the current title of which, *Intuitive Thinking as a Spiritual Path*, reflects its "spiritual" rather than its "philosophical" aspects.

Such distinctions, however, besides being obviously inadequate, are further confused by the highly individual nature of Steiner's works. As Steiner himself explicitly stated, his account in *The Philosophy of Freedom* did not seek to be universal, but only to map out for himself how he, the individual Rudolf Steiner, had walked that path. That is, each person, as Kühlewind did, must make it his own.

What makes *The Philosophy of Freedom* and the meditative path arising from it so radical (and so different from many other paths) is its implicit starting point.

It starts where we are, with ordinary thinking consciousness and our given faculties of sensing, feeling, and willing. On this basis, it proceeds by a meditative, step-by-step process of increasing phenomenological self-awareness to an intensification of our cognitive capacities; that is, a metamorphosis of consciousness. Then, after a while, and if we persevere, the process may unfold further until it reaches a moment when we experience a new sense of self—the true Self or "I am." Therewith a new world opens before us, the real world: the world of love.

And then, of course, the real work begins: to make those "I am" moments continuous and transformative of the world.

Starting where we are, we begin with our ordinary thinking. We notice that we never experience thinking, but only finished thoughts, finished concepts. We only experience the past; we do not experience the coming into being of thinking in the present. As Steiner puts it: "There are two things which are incompatible with each other: active production and objective contemplation." A boundary or wall seems to separate us from experiencing the "empty" consciousness from which by intuition thoughts and concepts arise. Consciousness for us is normally only finished thoughts, finished concepts, finished feelings, and finished perceptions. We are not aware of their coming into being; and so we never truly understand them. As for will, it is completely outside ordinary consciousness.

Hence, our primary experience is always of the continual loss of the present. What we experience—not only of thinking, but also of perceiving, feeling, and willing—is always falling into the past: into duality. The first task is to experience these in the present, in their process; that is, in the processes of cognition, perception, feeling, and willing.

Doing so, we realize the full import of the reality that the world is always the cognized, perceived, felt, and willed world: a non-dual world that we split—or is split by our "ego" or "me" consciousness—into subject-object, self-other, friend-enemy, humanity-nature, and so on.

To walk this path then is to heal the divide, which is the egotism that condemns us to the automatic repetition of the past. It is to learn to live in the present, that is, to love: to become spontaneously, improvisatorially creative of what is not yet, the future.

To this path, and the teaching of it, Georg Kühlewind dedicated his life. After his experience in 1958, as he puts it: "he slowly began the process of inner schooling." In 1964, he realized the importance of concentration exercises. He began daily concentration exercises (on a pair of ivory chopsticks), which continued until he died in January 2006. He began to work with small groups of friends and fellow spiritual seekers in 1965, and in 1966 to lecture in Austria, Switzerland, and Germany. Very early, he was led to meditate on the Logos, "the Word" in the beginning, as hymned by John the Evangelist in the Prologue to his Gospel. For twenty years or so, the first seventeen verses of John were his central meditation. Another key turning point came in 1969, when he met the Italian anthroposophist and *homo excersens*, or "exercising human being," Massimo Scaligero. In 1981 he retired, and from then on he dedicated himself exclusively to inner and philosophical work.

In more than twenty books, he laid out theoretical and practical prerequisites for the inner path. At the same time, he always worked intensively with small groups. At first, his work seemed more theoretical, more philosophical, but over the years it became clear to him that inner work was something one did, not something to talk about. Thus, he honed and experimented with a new, cognitive method of meditation.

*The Light of the "I,"* which is the last thing he wrote, is the ripe fruit of more than forty years of continuous practice. Summarizing and laying out the path of meditation that he himself walked, it is, in a certain sense, his testament. He had spent many years writing a book a year. The books he wrote, which were the results of his research—his meditations—will always be read (and meditated) for their profound spiritual and philosophical insights. But what was really important for him was that each one of us do the work for ourselves. Nothing was more important to him than that human beings should start meditating.

There are, perhaps, different ways of meditating. Certainly there are different ways of talking about meditation. The language we use to describe what we do when we meditate inevitably and implicitly frames our view of meditation and our expectations of it in a special way. It gives it a color and feel: a taste of its own.

Kühlewind's path, delineated in this book, has its own flavors, which will not necessarily or immediately seem to be to everyone's taste. One should not be overhasty in drawing such conclusions. I would plead that you give it a chance. Too often, we are drawn to a path because the first flavor we encounter is sympathetic to us: it makes us feel good. Likewise, when the first impression does not immediately draw us in, we tend to turn away. In both cases, we are seduced into overlooking the deeper, more fundamental flavors. Thus, all too frequently, it happens that, after a while, we experience disappointment. We cease practicing that particular path (and miss what it has to offer us), and, later, try another path. But what will we have missed? The point is always to keep going until the deeper flavors, the rewards, become evident.

Kühlewind's tone is serious. It is matter-of-fact. Every word counts and each sentence, whose simplicity is deceiving, must be thought through and pondered many times before being meditated. In other words, there are assumptions. Kühlewind takes it for granted that we are already on the path and that we recognize that a spiritual path is a path of consciousness: a cognitive path.

And so, in this little book, he proposes that we take up a program of "consciousness-training."

Therefore, his tone is injunctive: DO THIS!

To this end, he presents us with a series of exercises, leading to meditations, which are also a kind of exercise. When we wish to become fit, strong, and physically energetic, we exercise and discipline our bodies; likewise, if we want our consciousness to be clear, strong, and true to its nature—and to the nature of being itself—we must learn how to exercise it. The analogy is, however, only approximate. Mind and body are one.

As one, they—that is, we—are consciousness and only consciousness. But consciousness must here be understood also to include "thinking," which, in turn, must be understood to include "feeling" and "willing," only a small and problematic subset of which has to do with what we ordinarily call logic or reason.

Kühlewind further assumes that we have learned from experience that, as beings of consciousness, we do not always function healthily or efficiently. We begin a program of physical exercise because we become aware of the stiffness, sluggishness, and plain unresponsiveness of our bodies. But if we pay attention to our consciousness, we will find it in worse shape. Instead of clarity, directness, openness, compassion, and love, we find a tissue of hindrances: prejudices, distractions, preconceptions, ready-made, already-thought thoughts and concepts, reactive feelings (which are always essentially some kind of self-feeling, and nothing to do with the other or the world), and, at the level of will, addictions, compulsions—a kind of black hole.

All of these, loosely speaking, constitute our everyday self or "ego," whose entire consciousness is focused solely on defending and reinforcing itself at the expense of any true knowledge either of the world or of ourselves.

Surely we are more and other than this.

The path that Kühlewind teaches through these exercises and meditations is a path of selflessness. It is the fruit of hard-won experience and suffering, no matter how simple he makes it seem. Above all, it is a path that seeks to awaken us to the true nature of consciousness and of our own true being: the "I am," light, and attention.

He invites us to take it.

# Foreword

THIS BOOK IS NOT ONLY MY WORK. A friend, Javier Lantero, took the initiative of inviting a group of us to join him over a number of years on an annual retreat in Spain. The goal was *to draft a short, easy-to-understand guide to inner work.*

The first aspect of the inner work was to be the realization of the Self or "I."

Attention, which is the central human spiritual faculty, can meet or experience *itself*. In this experience, the witness, who is always present, awakens in self-awareness. This experience is the experience of the Self or "I." The second, related aspect of our work was to experience the miraculous nature of the Light, which, as "inner light," is called *attention*.

Attention enters into various forms, thoughts, images, and so on. All of these are *made up* of attention and all *appear*. They light up in the same single attention, which always experiences itself in the form of its contents. Ordinarily, we do not experience this miracle. We don't realize that we do not need another attention in order to experience these contents.

I would be happy if readers could participate in the presence of the light.

The paragraphs are numbered. Concentrated thinking may understand them individually and in their sequence. At the same time, they are content for meditation. Each may be expanded or deepened by meditation.

*Georg Kühlewind*

*(L'attention est la prière naturelle que nous faisons a la vérité intérieure, afin qu'elle se découvre en nous.)*

NICOLAS MALEBRANCHE, *Conversations chrétiennes*

*

Attention is the natural prayer we make to inner truth
in order that it may be revealed in us.

NICOLAS MALEBRANCHE, *Christian Conversations*

## What are we looking for?

1. Look at the sky. Do you see it? Look at the clouds. Do you see them?

2. Think: "The sky is blue." Think: "The clouds are white."

3. As long as your gaze is fixed on the blue sky, you cannot see the clouds.

As long as your gaze is fixed on a cloud, you cannot see the sky.

As long as you think, "The sky is blue," you cannot think anything else.

As long as you think, "The clouds are white," you cannot think anything else.

4. Whatever you think or see, your thinking or seeing is immersed in the form of your experience of thinking or seeing.

5. Your thinking or seeing attention has to withdraw from one form, and become form-free, in order to take up another form: the next experience.

6. During the transition from one experience to the next, attention has to be form-free, or empty.

7. Try to observe how attention *becomes* the image of the sky, or the clouds, this thought, this text.

8. When we try to observe how attention becomes an object, we experience that we cannot find the form-free attention but always find only formed states: the sky, the thoughts that we call the "objects" of attention.

9. Nevertheless, form-free attention must be there. It must be available to us. Otherwise, we could not experience different objects, thoughts, or feelings one after the other.

10. Attention seems to "mediate" what we perceive. But *what* is to be mediated? If we imagine something "objective" that could be mediated, it is already *in* our attention: it is an image that is made of attention.

11. Whatever we meet is actually a metamorphosis of our attention: a form of our attention. Similarly, whatever enters our awareness is an image or an experience that has arisen from our attention. Without attention, experience is impossible. This attention is our consciousness: our awareness or mind (spirit).

12. All objects, appearances, and forms come from, and may lead back to, the form-free empty mind or consciousness, whose metamorphoses they are.

13. There are things that seem to us to exist independently of our attention. But what exists for us—what is there for us—must appear to us, otherwise we would not know about it. This appearance takes place in our attention.

14. Attention is neither "outside" nor "inside." What could it be within? What could it be outside? Every "what"— every "something"— is itself already an appearance.

## Recapitulation

Attention can take only one form at a time. The form may be complex, but it is always a unity. Dispersed attention oscillates, bounces, or jumps from one unity to another.

All things, thoughts, or phenomena that we meet—what enters our consciousness, what we become aware of—*are* attention, conformed to what we meet.

We are "asleep"—not conscious—in the process of a thing's appearing. We wake up only when it has already appeared. Hence, we mistakenly believe that it is independent of our consciousness or attention.

The forms change. Form-free, empty attention must exist, but we do not experience it in everyday life.

15. Between our changing thoughts and changing perceptions there are holes in awareness, although we do not notice them. They are holes precisely because we do not notice them.

16. In these holes, our awareness is empty, and therefore can enter into the next form. The processes, which generate cognition, understanding, thoughts and so on, occur in the holes. In these processes we are not conscious. We are asleep, and only become aware of the finished, formed products.

17. The holes are like a capacity to produce forms. The capacity to paint, for instance, is empty. It is form-free in comparison to the images that originate from it and come about by it.

18. Compared to its products, the empty capacity is the greater reality. In the same way, when compared with its contents, the empty attention or consciousness is the more powerful reality.

19. The greater reality of empty attention or consciousness is usually not experienced as such: we are not aware of it.

20. The whole world emerges in and through awareness. Without awareness, there is no experience. When our attention drifts away, our eyes do not see and our ears do not hear.

21. The known world is the content of our attention. Attention, therefore, is the fundamental reality. And we do not experience it.

22. Nor do we experience the forming of the concepts, percepts, and cognitions by which we know the world.

They come about through the supra-conscious form-free attention.

23. We do not experience the greater part of the world—of what may be called reality. We have a false image of the world. The first reason to try to realize form-free attention is because we want to have a more accurate image of the world.

24. What we call "I" or "me" in everyday life is a feeling around the body and (if an organ is not functioning properly) in the body. This "I" or "me" is the object of our attention; therefore we can know about it. Somewhere, somehow, the true subject (of these observations) must be hidden within the observing attention. The second reason why we seek the experience of form-free attention is thus because we want to find this hidden subject.

25. The true subject or Self cannot be an object, for this would presuppose or require another subject.

26. If we could experience form-free attention, we would have the means of attaining the true Self. We would receive more insights, ideas and understandings. But this can happen only in an empty mind or an empty state of attention. To become more intuitive or improvisatory is thus the third reason why we seek the experience of free attention.

27. As indicated, empty attention is what makes possible the experiencing of anything at all. It is always present but hidden in us. It is always potentially at our disposal.

28. We need only find the way to experience it consciously.

## *Summary*

We do not experience that through which we experience everything else. We know more or less what we do when we tie our shoelaces. We do not know how we think, remember, or speak. Therefore we do not know how we encounter the world. We do not know what reality, the world, or human beings, are. It is not surprising then that, as individuals and as human beings, we experience serious problems in life.

Zen Buddhists and early Christians saw the situation clearly. Both had the experience of form-free attention as their goal. Zen called this experience seeing the innate Buddha-nature; Christians called it experiencing the Light or Inner Light.

29. Because of the constitution of our mind, we are surrounded by a world of objects. Even our thoughts and inner images are objects of an observing (perceiving) attention.

30. To say that we do not experience empty attention is the same as to say that we never become aware of thinking in the present, but only of thoughts: that is, past thinking. This is true for perceptions as well. If they are apprehended conceptually, they appear ready-made. We do not experience the process of their appearing.

31. The empty or form-free mind, the source of all our experiences, cannot be achieved by using thinking and concepts; which just cover up their own origin.

32. The normal direction of the flow of attention is the following: originating from an unknown, supra-conscious source, attention is not experienced until it reaches an object. This is what becomes conscious.

33. Therefore, the empty mind must be found before the object. It must be found before form-free attention turns into its object-form. As with every discovery, this one too could be sudden, not gradual: a flash, a glimpse of light.

34. Concentrated attention is focused only on one object; dispersed attention jumps around quickly and touches many objects.

35. To withdraw attention from its objects, to cease to use concepts or to experience differences, is possible only when attention is concentrated, or bundled. If our attention is split, we have no means of withdrawing it, piece by piece, from separate objects.

36. People today cannot withdraw attention from its objects, because their attention is not sufficiently concentrated.

37. Objects are forms with which attention was briefly identical—without our experiencing the identity. They are lost moments of identity.

38. When we lose the moment of identity, the objects or finished forms become experiences of the past. Because the past can be experienced only out of the present, the present witness begins to appear. The appearance of the present witness first occurs, for the moment, in abstraction, as a thought, or simply in reflection.

39. Because the greatest reality, empty mind or consciousness, is neither outside nor inside, there is nothing to attain, nothing to strive for, and no object to be achieved.

40. Only one kind of practice is needed—to intensify attention—for the simple reason that only concentrated attention, concentrated consciousness or awareness can become empty.

41. The mind or awareness that experiences is always empty. Only empty awareness or consciousness can change into forms—and it is always changing its forms. What we seek is present, as a gift, from the beginning.

42. At a certain point of concentration, we feel ourselves becoming the object on which we are concentrating. We identify with its function (which we have to know). But then, of course, it is no longer an object. At first, we experience identity for only brief moments, after which we fall again and again outside the object. But after a while we are able to remain identified with the object for longer periods. Then we no longer "see" the image from outside, but enter into it.

## Recapitulation

We seem to be surrounded by a world of objects, an objective world, because the process of the world's appearing remains unconscious—supraconscious. We encounter only the finished results of the process. We wake up when the world has already appeared. If we could experience the world's process of appearing, we would experience a different, more complete reality. Phenomena become reality if they are experienced as the metamorphosis of the empty mind. Otherwise they remain illusion, or *maya*.

43. Any differentiation occurs through an undifferentiated agent or power. Time is experienced as differentiated: that is, as earlier or later.

44. The form-free state of the mind is beyond time. Time is the result of the steady and repeated process of falling out of timeless emptiness. Even meanings are timeless. The mind's changing from meaning to meaning—not experiencing everything at once or simultaneously—generates time.

45. We do not experience the processes of the mind; we experience only when they halt or stop. Where the continuous understanding comes to a halt, a concept arises.

46. We call what seems to be independent of our consciousness "outside." What is within our consciousness, we call "inside." But what is outside is also conscious. If it were not, we would not know about it. We lack only awareness of the process through which it appears.

47. We cannot avoid consciousness or light. There may be a way—however difficult—to avoid objects.

48. There is no way to avoid the "I," regardless of what we experience. Whether we speak of it or do not speak of it, we are either aware of a witness, or we are asleep. But to know this, we must be awake.

49. When we meet a sign or word for the first time, we must understand its meaning, which we usually call a "concept." Thereafter, words and texts substitute for concepts and ideas. Concepts and ideas take the place of unbroken understanding. The first time we meet them, concepts are experienced. They are understood. Thereafter they are merely used.

50. To experience understanding before something is understood is the experience of empty attention. This empty attention is understanding itself. It enables us to understand.

51. When we understand something, the power of understanding, which in itself is form-free, takes on the form of the understood.

52. When we see something, the power of seeing, which in itself is form-free, becomes the form of the seen.

53. Attention is always self-experiencing. First, it experiences itself in the forms made of it; then it experiences itself as flowing into the forms; then it experiences itself as form-free, empty awareness.

54. Can the world and its appearing be distinguished? Where does the world appear?

## Recapitulation

There can be no phenomena without formed attention. There can be no formed attention without empty attention, which is light. There can be no attention at all, if it is not the attention of someone, the witness to the phenomena, the one who is experiencing them. Whenever we speak of something, there is a phenomenon, an attention, and a witness, but usually we become aware only of the phenomenon. We forget the light behind it, by which we become aware of it; and we forget the "I"-being, who becomes aware of it.

The last named—the light and the "I"— are usually not experienced. Free attention is the spiritual part of the soul. Until we experience form-free attention, we are psychological beings; but when we experience form-free attention, we are spiritual beings. Form-free attention is tuned to understanding: that is, it is tuned to take up the form of a meaning.

What we look for is not a teaching. It is not words, concepts, theories, or information. It is not a worldview. It is an experience.

A faculty—from which all faculties arise—leads us to the experience. It is the faculty to see the whole process—the phenomenon, the attention and the witness—as a unity.

# EXERCISES

## *First, Some Advice*

All exercises should be carried out with a "soft," relaxed, playful will. There should be no pressure or compulsion to achieve results. If one simply does the exercises, one will find that, after a few attempts, they will succeed.

To access the soft will, concentrate your feeling-attention on parts of the body. Try to feel them lightly: the top of the head, the forehead, the neck, the shoulders and shoulder blades, along the spine, the chest, the stomach, and so on. Or, imagine a peaceful scene: blue sky, white clouds sailing slowly across it; or a pond with a slowly, quietly swimming swan etc.

## *The Basic Exercise*
### *(suggested by Dr. Hartwig Volbehr)*

Once we are relaxed, we are ready to do the Basic Exercise, which should precede any other exercise. It should be done for about ten minutes a day, independently of other exercises.

If we observe ourselves in daily life, we will notice that very often, indeed for the most part, we *react*, which means there is no pause or gap between "input" and "output," and that our actions are causally conditioned. Automatisms, enervations, habits, prejudices, preconceived and habitual opinions act, not us. Something happens to us and immediately we do something, without reflection or consideration, as if we were acting in a causal chain.

The Basic Exercise consists in putting a short break between what happened and our response to it, as if we said to ourselves: "Just one moment, please." This instantly *cuts off the causal chain* of which we seem to be part. It realizes a *free moment*.

A "free moment" is a moment of *beginning* or creativity (for no true creation has a reason or cause). The practice of the "free moment" can be developed to the point or moment when the mind is *free of concepts*. Then a new idea may appear.

When it is without concepts, the free moment is the first step to *cognitive feeling*.

Preparing the way to the *intuitive moment* in any sense perception, it helps us achieve the experience of form-free or *empty attention*.

At first, a free moment may last a few seconds; then it can grow shorter; until it ends up needing no time at all: like the flash of understanding that does not happen in time.

In addition to our daily practice of ten minutes, this exercise should be done before any other exercise. Every exercise should be preceded by a moment of silence and peace. If we do it at a convenient time every day, the "free moment" may expand to include any of our actions; and so we may avoid some of the inconsiderate deeds or situations into which we may otherwise slip.

Walter Benjamin, the German philosopher, wrote: "Every moment is a small door through which the Messiah could enter."

## Concentration Exercise

55. Our attention can actually focus only on *one* theme at a time; but everyday life compels us to be attentive to many themes simultaneously, and so we are used to doing so. This happens because we move the beam of our attention quickly from one theme to another, as if we were directing the beam of a flashlight.

56. To balance this kind of scattered attention, we try to focus on *one* inner image of a simple, familiar, man-made thing like a paperclip, a pin, a needle, a pencil, or a ring etc.

57. What we focus on should not be attractive. If it were attractive, holding its image would not come about by our will. The object of our focus should be "man-made," because that means that we know its function, which is closely connected with its concept. We do not know the function or concept of natural things.

58. The inner image is easily summoned by the question: "What does it look like?" Or, better, addressing the thing from the beginning: "What do *you* look like?"

59. Addressing our "man-made" object with the question "What do *you* look like?" we achieve a whole, a complete image of the object. But if we "construct" it

part by part, we see only the part that we are working on.

60. In the same way, we can also summon "fantasy images" like a three-headed dragon.

61. This exercise can be done with eyes either closed or open. We should do whichever is easier for us. If our eyes are open, however, we must avoid looking at anything. Also, as far as possible, we must try to avoid thinking during the exercise.

62. When we see the image of the chosen object with our inner eyes, we try to hold the image for a few minutes. Since the image is volatile, we speak to it. For example, we address it, saying inwardly: "Stay," "No hurry," "We have time." What we say is irrelevant. Only addressing the object is important.

63. We must not address the object superficially, but seriously, focused upon the image with intense attention. After a few attempts, we will no longer need to use many words or whole sentences. Inwardly uttering a syllable, like "Hi" or "Hmm," or a whistle will suffice.

64. The final form in which we address the object is our *gaze*. We use an addressing gaze to visualize the image. As long as we address it, it cannot vanish.

65. In proportion to its intensity, the gaze we address the image with protects the mind from distractions. The gaze and its intensity indicate that that we are in control of the object, because we know how to focus the gaze,

no matter what happens in our imagination. We can do whatever we want with the object or its image.

*Disturbances that can arise during the exercises:*

*The image does not appear.* In this case, don't try to "see" the image with your eyes; that is, on the inner side of the eyelids. Place the image of the thing on a table, or somewhere in front of you (perhaps even behind you). If you still have difficulty visualizing it, make up a little story about your object. For example, you have lent it to a friend and he or she has just returned it. The moment you receive it, you will "see" it. Or you have lost the object (sometimes this already leads to "seeing" it), and you find it in a corner of the room or among a heap of other objects. Finding it, you "see" it.

*The image moves.* Don't worry; try to quiet it down; and, if it keeps moving, simply observe its movements. Or begin the exercise again. Whatever happens to the image, observe it. If the experience moves toward identification—the object comes closer; it becomes bigger—let it happen. Don't force the visualization into duality, into seeing it from "outside"—that happens anyway in your mind.

*The image disappears.* In this case, ask it: "What do you look like?" Address it.

*Distractions, associations, other images enter.* Don't fight them; try to ignore them; return to the theme.

"Back to the theme" is always the motto in any case.

If the associations are tenacious, invite them in, and observe them from the side, looking at them as they appear and change; and then, from time to time, try to return to the theme.

Even if there is no thinking without images and no imaging without thinking, thinking and imaging are not compatible. When we visualize, we must try as far as possible to diminish thinking by intensifying the imagining gaze—never by suppressing thinking.

If we practice simple visualizations lasting a few minutes, the exercise will change spontaneously, and to a great extent individually, as the intensity of our attention increases. What we do next depends on the direction our attention takes. We can turn to the form or function or idea of our chosen thing.

## Playing with Attention

a) Imagine an image; hold it for a short time (as described in 58 and 64); then let it fade away by ceasing to address it with the inner gaze. After letting associations enter, recall the image. Repeat these two movements several times.

b) Do a), but try to observe what your attention is doing, or what is happening to it, during the operation. Let the image vanish in a cloud of mist and then let it emerge out of the cloud.

c) Repeat the previous exercise, but now let the mist come out of the object. The object begins—say, at one end—to evaporate into mist, and then dissolves completely into the mist, which is now the metamorphosed object. Now let the object reappear as coming out of the mist. If you have difficulty imagining the mist, imagine it to be colored.

d) Choose three objects. They can be of the same kind, like three spoons of different sizes, or three different kinds of objects. First, imagine the mist; then let the first object appear out of it. Hold it for it a short while; then let it return again into the mist. Now let the second object arise out of the mist; hold it for a short while; then let it become mist again. Do the same with the third object.

e) Imagine the object; hold the image for a short while; then (1) let the imagined object become more and more light-filled, as if glowing; (2) let it dissolve into light; (3) let it reappear into its light-filled form; and finally (4), let it return into the form that it had at the beginning of the exercise. (Again, if you experience any difficulty, give the light a color.)

f) Repeat exercise d), but instead of mist use light.

g) Imagine a blue cloudless sky with the radiant light-filled disc of the sun. Let the sun expand into the whole sky, so that the blue disappears. Let the object appear from this light-filled sky and then disappear again. Then let the light withdraw into the disc of the sun, so you have the initial image of the blue sky and the sun again.

66. The form of a thing can awaken feelings. A straight line produces a different feeling than a wavy line; a triangle is different in feeling from a circle. Follow the lines of a thing. No words can describe the feelings aroused. These cognitive feelings may be supported by other qualities of the thing we imagine—like color, brightness, and tactile quality. (Suggested by Javier Lantero.)

67. The form is determined by the function. Imagine the thing in its function. The function is will-like, because its inventor followed a will, that is, that the thing should function just as it does. No words can describe this will.

68. The idea of the thing is what its inventor's "saw" with his or her "inner eyes." If our concentration is sufficiently intense, we will receive the idea of our thing: a wordless, image-less, pure *"that."* Do not try to reach it. Only strengthen your concentration. In your mind the idea is yours to do with what you will. With its help, we could invent the thing anew.

69. If we do this exercise regularly (a least once a day), our attention will grow in intensity, even when we do not practice; we will become more concentrated human beings. Up to a critical point in the exercise, we must strive for continuity of attention. Our attention must not weaken or become distracted. This depends on the power of address.

70. Once we attain a certain degree of intensity, which is impossible to define, our attention begins and continues to grow by itself, without our care and effort. Attention

is then directed healthily toward one thing. To be one-pointed is attention's original and healthy nature.

71. We can now have two further experiences. First, we can feel ourselves identified with the object, with its function or idea.

72. Second, at the same time, or by slightly more growth, our attention can experience itself flowing into the theme, bringing about the theme, but still in a form-free state.

73. *This experience we call the "I-am" experience.* It is the universal healing medicine. It is a feeling of identity with an ever-deepening being that wills itself. It provides certainty, creativity, and solidity, and dissolves what comes from egotism. From it, the knowledge arises that nothing can happen to me (the one who is experiencing this): I am safe, completely independent of circumstances, opinions, successes or failures. I have found my spiritual roots.

## Explanations

a) At the beginning of the exercise, we produce a high intensity of attention, which usually decreases in the course of time, depending on our power of address. As it declines, the intensity begins to undulate. It rises and sinks, rises and sinks (just as our waking consciousness does when are falling asleep). When it does so, we know—if we do not, by an act of will, renew attention—that in the next moment we will be distracted, that is, something will enter our awareness without or against our will. By not renewing our attention, we consent to the distraction.

b) We know the experience of identification because we have occasionally experienced it in the theatre, at a concert, or viewing a beautiful landscape. In these cases, identification occurs because of the attractiveness of what we are experiencing. For a fraction of a second, attention becomes—that is, we become—identical with anything that enters our awareness: perceptions, thoughts, images etc. In the exercise, the identity is prolonged. Hence it can be experienced. In the exercise, identification usually comes about in the flow of attention toward the object. As the intensity of attention increases, identification changes in quality from thinking or imagining: first, into feeling-attention; then into willing-attention, which each time is "further away" from the "object-picture" we started with, and closer to its supra-conscious origin.

c) The "I-am" experience makes it clear that attention is the possibility of the real self, which is not the "me-feeling" that we call "me" in everyday life. The "I-am" experience is the experience of the empty, not-yet formed attention, as it itself becomes aware. It is the first spiritual experience. It is a non-dualistic experience, just as identification is—as if a beam of water became illuminated from within.

## Self-forgetting

We can forget ourselves in an emotion and do something we repent later. We can forget ourselves in associations, in daydreaming, in fantasies. Such self-forgetting lowers our wakefulness and lets consciousness slip below its everyday level.

We can forget ourselves when we do the concentration exercise, for example when we enter or become the image. Because the image is made by us, and is made of our attention, the "me" is forgotten in this kind of self-forgetting and the self itself becomes active. Forgetting the "me" provides the opportunity to wake up as an "I-am."

## Two Special Exercises

a. Do a concentration exercise (55-65). Turn your first gaze after finishing it onto a tree, a bunch of flowers, or a human face. Observe your experience in the first seconds, or fraction of a second, before thinking begins to work. Objects then look different than they usually do.

b. Having done a concentration exercise—being concentrated—we look at something in the room, like a simple object some distance away (such as a lamp, cushion, vase, or cup, etc.). We begin the look with the feeling or thought: "that there." If our seeing is concentrated, the experience of the object may change into "this here." The object appears to come closer, or we become identical with it.

## Becoming Vertical (Upright)

To join the human community and meet the world, a child becomes vertical (upright) in a human environment. Were we to live horizontally, we would be part of the world without witnessing it.

Before it experiences itself, attention is supraconscious. Symbolically, we could imagine attention to originate from above, and flow vertically downward. The "me," on the other hand, can direct its attention only horizontally, i.e., toward objects. Thus, ordinary, everyday attention loses its original verticality. It becomes "broken" and horizontal. "We look around." Although we always have the vertical direction of attention at our disposal, we remain unaware of it before it turns into objects, and so cannot use it with our everyday ("me") will to receive new thoughts or ideas.

In the intervals or pauses between the changing objects of attention, our "me"-feeling is touched. Attention oscillates between the object and the "me." But if attention becomes one-pointed and unmoving (in concentration and meditation), forgetting the "me," it turns back to the vertical. It becomes our spiritual spine. Becoming vertical and intense, attention can detach itself from the object or theme. It can become empty, pure light, self-conscious, a Self, connected with its source. The New Testament calls it the individualized Holy Spirit, sent by the Lord.

Meditation uses vertical attention. It lifts awareness into the vertical. It makes it aware of meditative contents without duality, in witnessed identity, and makes the theme transparent to its higher meaning.

## Results of Concentration and Summary

74. In the exercises we try to retrieve the original functioning of attention, such as is found in small children and in archaic cultures. Such attention arises from a supraconscious source and is directed toward an object. The directedness forms and strengthens the spine of our awareness.

75. As we become more experienced in the exercise, we can work with distractions in a different way. Instead of trying to avoid them, we can try to see them as unwanted metamorphoses of our attention. If we succeed in doing so, we can withdraw the stream of attention from them and turn it back to the theme.

76. The experience of identity with the theme enables us to realize the *bridge*—namely, the attention that connects subject and object, which usually we do not notice. Experiencing that the theme is made of attention is the experience of identity. Subject and object become one. Later, we can experience this bridge in any content of our consciousness.

77. Leaving behind or erasing the theme does not result in the attainment of empty attention. Empty attention is attained *before* the theme, before the stream of form-free attention turns into the theme. It brings it about.

78. The witnessing Self can use this form-free attention as the receptive attention for new intuitions.

79. If the theme is not a "man-made" object, but a symbol that stands for a meaning, which cannot be communicated

as information, the exercise changes somewhat and is called *meditation*. In concentration, the "meaning" of the object is known. In meditation, we are looking for "meanings" beyond the informational meaning we understand.

Once we begin to meditate, we achieve the only really fully free deed possible in this human life....
When we meditate, we are completely free.

RUDOLF STEINER, *Lecture on August 8, 1922*

# MEDITATION

80. Information can be understood without the person receiving it having to create new concepts. But there are also experiences, which resist being communicated as information. They are themes for meditation.

81. Such experiences (that resist being communicated as information) can be put into forms that lead the mind that is concentrated on them to the experience from which they originate.

82. In receiving or creating information and informational texts, thinking moves discontinuously from known concept to known concept. The movement is exhausted every time it reaches a known concept and stops there. Everyday attention has to move in order to be sustained.

83. We do not seek thinking, but not-thinking. That is to say, we seek to return to the pure power of empty thinking attention. Meditation, even when it is directed attention onto a theme, is not-thinking.

84. If we not-think, our thinking power is unmoving, quiet, still. It works continuously, which is the same as staying still.

85. Being really attentive does not mean thinking, or feeling, or even becoming the receptive will. Attention remains unmoving on the theme. It avoids concepts, thoughts, and anything already-formed. It remains fluid thinking that is form-free and concept-building.

86. This attention is the light that penetrates everything—because everything is made of this light.

87. Meditation themes are the true objects of attention: unthinkable, and therefore transmissible and transparent to meditation. The self can turn the empty, as-yet-unformed attention onto them.

88. If attention is not sufficiently concentrated, the mind falls back into thinking. All kinds of meditations imply training and increased attention.

## Text Meditation— Returning to Signless, Wordless Meaning

89. Every sentence, and every sequence of sentences, originates from a core—a *"that"*—which is beyond language, beyond signs.

90. This core, which is the meaning, enables the mind to find the right words and grammatical forms, which are the signs. The meaning is beyond language. It is what can be translated from one language into another. To create or understand an informational sentence, we must—for a moment, a flash—attain the signless, wordless meaning.

91. Meditative sentences contain a hidden meaning behind the obvious, translatable, informational meaning. In meditation, we try to reach this hidden meaning by concentrating the unmoving attention on the informational meaning.

92. As attention, when it is concentrated, can have only one theme, the first difficulty in meditating is that a sentence is constituted of more words than one, and that the informational meaning is already hidden in the words making up the sentence.

93. Therefore we try to reduce the sentence to its core, to its origin, which preceded the words. If attention is sufficiently intense, we can do it immediately; or we can do it by condensing the sentence into one of its words; or even into one word not taken from the sentence.

94. We choose a word—say, the one that seems to be the most important or that seems most sympathetic to us—and bring the meaning of the other words one after the other into our chosen word, which will then represent the whole sentence.

95. Then we have only *one* sign, one word, upon which we can concentrate our unmoving, not-thinking attention. Depending on the power of our attention, the last sign (word) may disappear, so that only pure, signless, wordless meaning remains.

96. The signless, wordless meaning may then become transparent and allow a new meaning to shine forth, one that is expressible only by a meditative sentence

or image. The appearing of a new—deeper or higher—meaning is an experience. Therefore, it is indubitable and certain.

97. When we repeat a meditation on the same theme, we experience—when successful—a second, deeper or higher, meaning, which does not contradict our first experience, but integrates or deepens it. Every meditation on a given theme provides a new meaning, because every experience changes us and, as our consciousness changes, the theme reveals a new essence.

## Technical Advice and Examples

It is best to begin our meditation by "pondering" the text or image: chewing it over with ever-deepening thinking. In a concentrated state, we think through the words and the structure of the sentence. The function of this concentrated reflection is to exhaust thinking. When our attention is focused in meditation, we should not be thinking. But thinking can help us enter meditation—as, for instance, when something new arises in the light of thinking.

Let us consider a standard Zen Buddhist meditation, "This Mind is Buddha," as an example of a meditation sentence.

First, we ponder about the word "This."

Ordinarily we use the word "this" to point to something close to us: closer than "that." But whatever we point to can only be called "that." There is only one thing, which cannot be "that," and only "this," namely: what we are doing just now. A moment later: "this" is already "that." If we can point at it, it is "that." "This," if we take it seriously, is therefore not a demonstrative pronoun. It does not point. What I do now, and where now is really experienced in everyday life, is identical with the "I"—which never can be "that."

Text meditation can thus be described in three steps:

1.) Pondering.

2.) Reduction (into one word or symbol).

3.) Concentration on the one symbol or the meaning—the real meditation.

There are other ways of "reducing" a sentence: for instance, by "gluing" together all the words of the sentence so that they make a unity.

Here is an example of reduction. We shall reduce "This Mind is Buddha" to a single word. We shall choose as our remaining word "This"—but any word may be chosen. Then, first, we put the meaning of "Mind" into "This"—*This* (Mind) *is Buddha.*" Then we condense the meaning of "Is" into "This"—*This* (Mind is) *Buddha.*" The last step is to allow whatever meaning we give to the word "Buddha" into "This"—*This* (Mind is Buddha).*" On this meaning-filled "This" (which represents the whole sentence), we now concentrate.

We can connect meditation with the concentration exercise by choosing an appropriate theme. This will still be a "man-made" thing, but one that has a symbolic meaning as well, like "key," "cup" or "chalice," "door," "string" and so on.

Beginning with concentration on the object, we reach the point of identity and the "I-am"-experience. Then, we consider the object as a symbol, and meditate on it in the same way that we meditate on a text: we take the informational (translatable) meaning as a symbol for the hidden meaning.

In meditation, the same transformations may occur as in the concentration exercise: the quality of attention first changes from thinking or representing into feeling, and then into receptive willing.

When we begin our meditative practice, we work with short, one-sentence texts. Later, we can turn to longer texts, so long as we can consider them as a unity or single statement: that is, as a single, if complex, meaning. In the case of a series of sentences, we can do the following: take the first sentence as the meditation-theme, and read or think the others after having meditated the first; then take the second sentence as the theme, and so on. Or after the first sentence, take the first and the second together as the theme for meditation, and so on.

98. When we experience a new meaning in our meditation, we realize that this new meaning was present from the beginning, from eternity, and that we needed only to open to it.

99. When our attention grows beyond the point of identity with what was previously its object—that is, with what was the pretext to arouse and keep it flowing—and beyond the experience of "I-am," it changes from thinking/imagining into feeling attention.

100. If we use conceptual thinking, which is robbed of its root in feeling, then feeling loses its task and turns into anxiety.

101. This anxiety disappears with the "I-am"-experience. The experience of identity goes over into the realm of feeling and goes deeper and deeper.

## Symbolic Image Meditation

### Introduction

102. Intuitive thinking usually turns into images produced by the intuitive process. So sentence-meditation consists primarily in providing images, which we translate into words.

103. Images are made of and irradiate feelings, because their elements do the same. A straight line irradiates a different feeling than a wavy line; a triangle feels different from a circle. The same holds true for colors and spatial forms.

104. The original feeling-perception that small children and archaic people possess does not need sense organs, and always happens directly: in identity, without dualism.

105. For the world to reach consciousness in portions, the senses split the feelable world into sense-qualities.

106. Nevertheless, if conceptual thinking did not intervene, a sense-specific feeling would penetrate to the mind through the senses.

107. To experience the feeling that irradiates from images, we have to get rid of concepts. Concepts immediately

bury what we perceive through the senses. Concepts kill feeling.

108. When we see an image (or thing), there is a momentary flash of feeling, which concepts then extinguish. Feeling is non-dualistic; conceptual perception is dualistic.

109. In imagining, we start from a conceptual sketch of the image. Then we try to overcome it, so as to advance to the feeling experience. Success depends on the intensity of attention. Attention can change into feeling simultaneously with the disappearance of the conceptual structure.

## Example of Image Meditation

In this example, the image is a dynamic one: a process. We imagine a sandy desert: sunny, hot, and parched. On one spot, a rose plant begins to appear: first, the stem, the leaves, a bud, and then a radiant red rose-flower.

110. Using the inner question, "What do you look like?" we try to "see" the desert as described above. We do not try to put the image together out of its parts.

111. With the same inner gesture, we let the rosebush grow out of the dry sand and unfold until the flower appears. As far as possible, we do not help the process of imagining such unreal or impossible situations by picturing or thinking "realistic" circumstances, such as hidden water or a well under the desert.

112. We hold the image—perhaps by speaking to it as in the concentration exercise. We concentrate on it with a questioning inner gesture: "What are you saying?" "What's your meaning?" Rather than using words, the questioning gesture should take place in feeling.

113. When concentration is sufficiently intense, the image will arouse a new, never-before-experienced feeling that is the "answer" to our question, "What are you saying?"

114. The new feeling may occur simultaneously with the image becoming transparent or dissolving; and it may be preceded by images or thoughts that are similar to the image on which we are meditating; or it may be preceded by situations that possess similarly unreal features.

115. Because it is unreal, it is difficult to let the rose in the desert grow. If, however, we succeed in creating a vivid image of the rose, the feeling corresponding to it will arise. We will have created a wonder, a miracle.

116. The more we succeed in simply "seeing," instead of circling around what has occurred in our thinking, the stronger will be the feeling that arises. As far as possible, we do not try to put the feeling into words.

117. If we do not succeed in imagining the plant in the desert, then we try to feel the impossibility, the obstacle.

118. The "meaning" of the image is in the feeling. Apart from the image, the feeling has no mediation.

119. We can experience this feeling-meaning only if we have built the bridge: the flow of conscious attention imprinted by the theme. In other words, only if we become identified with the image.

120. Since the image is the direct sign of the meaning (which is not conventional, as letters are for sounds), the mind's (or consciousness's) identity with the image is the same as its identity with the meaning. Therefore we "understand" in feeling.

### Static Image Examples for Beginning Image Meditation

A circle without, then with, a center point.
A triangle without, then with, a center point.
Buddha holding and showing a flower in his left hand.
A garden, enclosed by a wall, with a closed door.

Themes for image-meditations may be found in the Bible. In the New Testament, for instance, all the parables are images. The central parable of the sower can be meditated to realize what the "Kingdom" means. Fairy tales, too, consist of images suitable for meditation. Having read the parables or the tales, we can choose or make an image that represents the whole text and meditate on it. For example, we may imagine the sower in the field.

## Perceptual Meditation

### Introduction

121. We do a concentration exercise. When we are finished, we cast our first glance at a thing, perhaps a flower, or a plant or a stone. Then, for a moment, we can see that the world looks different than it usually does.

122. We can become conscious when we contemplate a human face with a holistic, feeling gaze. On the basis of this kind of holistic gaze, we can recognize a person or recall their face as an inner image without knowing any of their individual features: for instance, what their nose looks like.

123. We can become conscious of how eye-contact differs from any other way of looking, especially from the searching gaze of doctor or scientist.

124. We look at a tree, a stone or a plant. We try to become aware that there are usually two components present: (1) a concept or concept-like thought and (2) sense-qualities, which sometimes have general names (like colors), and sometimes are nameless (like shades of color or the irregular forms of leaves or stones).

125. When looking at (or contemplating) a work of art or a beautiful landscape, we can experience a phase of pure dedication when the process of making a conceptual inventory comes to a complete stop.

126. We can observe how, in everyday perception, attention oscillates with tremendous speed between the states of dedication and conceptualization—that is, "naming" what is perceived.

127. In the first moments of perception following a concentration exercise, conceptual thinking is still quiet and unmoving, and the world looks different than it usually does.

128. Usually, we perceive conceptually. It is difficult, if not impossible, to experience pure perception, devoid of concepts.

129. As long as attention oscillates between dedication and thinking, we cannot experience the "bridge" of attention that simultaneously connects and dissolves subject and object: the unmoving attention.

130. When conceptual thinking stops or pauses, the feeling behind thinking regains its power. We know that if we are able to keep thinking stilled, feeling perception will be reactivated.

131. Because it uses concepts, everyday perception attains only the informational meaning of what it perceives. We are happy if we simply know what it is. But even to attain this information takes a moment of dedication; otherwise we would perceive nothing. When attention is busy with other themes, the senses will not be active.

132. The need for dedication, which is unnecessary when we imagine an image, originates in the fact that in

perception there is something given, which is not of our doing, not even in the sense that the content of thinking is our choice. We can think anything we want to, even if the process of thinking is supraconscious; but we cannot perceive in the same way. What we perceive has "to be there."

133. A natural thing can be seen as the activity or "work" of Nature. Formed by a power, it irradiates this power by its form (and all its qualities).

134. In everyday perception we receive a complicated mixture of Nature's "work" and our "work," which includes both conceptualization and subjective feelings of sympathy and antipathy.

*Exercises*

135. The aim of the preparatory exercise (for perceptual meditation) is to separate the components of ordinary perception. Using receptive attention, we try to get the power irradiated by natural objects in the purest possible form. We try to allow our receptive attention to be imprinted by the power that the objects irradiate.

136. As the subject of the exercise we take a pebble, one for which we feel no special sympathy or antipathy. We look at it as a whole, as far as possible without concepts, for about a half a minute. Then we close our eyes or put aside the pebble, and try to imagine what we have seen—if necessary, using the question "What do you look like?" Then we try to keep the image again for about a half a minute.

137. We repeat this exercise (136) several times, suc-cessively shortening the time we take to look at it initially, so that in the end we just become momentarily aware of the stone. If we are sufficiently concentrated, contrary to what we expect, our imagining will be the most vivid after the shortest look, for the same reason as mentioned in #127.

138. Exercises 136 and 137 should be done for relatively long periods: once or twice a day for at least three weeks. Following this, we try to do exercise 139.

139. We look at our pebble twice, differently each time. First, we look at it with a detailed, searching, analytic gaze: we try to experience the pebble's individual details. This "scientific" gaze is accompanied by the feeling that a stream (of attention) flows from me to the stone. After about half a minute of this look, we blink once or twice. This is done to separate the first phase of the exercise from the next. Then we look again. But this time we use a soft, receptive, inviting, holistic gaze—such as we use in eye-contact with someone. This is accompanied by the feeling that something now streams from the stone to us. We invite the pebble in feeling, inwardly feeling "Show yourself," "Speak," "Tell your wordless story." We remain in this second gaze for up to five minutes—as long as we continue to experience a difference between the first and the second gaze. As far as possible, we try not to verbalize any experience we have had during the second gaze.

## Possible Experience (during exercise 139)

We experience no difference between the two gazes. If this happens, we return to exercises 136 and 137 for another week. This negative experience may have several causes:

a. Thinking, concepts, or words may come up during the second gaze and interfere with our receptive gesture. This means that thinking is not yet sufficiently disciplined. In this case, we return to the thinking/imagining concentration exercises on a "man-made" object (56-64) in order to strengthen the "I," so that it can bear the mighty ideas that are the "meaning" of natural phenomena.

b. We feel moved during the second gaze. This is a positive experience, but we should not give in to it too deeply. It touches us to be close to mighty ideas, which, perhaps for the first time, we feel are realities. Or, we begin to feel our connection with the reality of our pebble.

140. This kind of meditation seems to be easy. It seems to lead to experiences the first time we do it. But the expectation of having the same experience, or indeed any expectation, makes subsequent attempts more difficult.

141. If we succeed in our meditation, and achieve with regularity the second, receptive gaze, we can begin to do variations of this exercise: for instance, comparing first and second looks at two different kinds of pebbles; then perhaps a pebble and a live leaf; then a pebble and a dead leaf; or two different leaves etc. Through such "comparisons" our feeling-sensitivity grows.

142. As the receptive attention grows, we can begin to experience the bridge—namely, how our receptive attention becomes imprinted by the object, which in the experience begins to cease to be an *object*.

143. As this experience intensifies, reality changes: the pebble, the seeing of it, and the witness become one reality.

144. The unity of attention and object is achieved in cognitive feeling. It is similar to when one begins to read the letters of the alphabet to reach to the meaning. Not to read means to remain outside of the meaning. To read is to enter into the meaning. Meaning is "outside" the higher meaning, if there is one, as in meditation themes. Higher meaning, in turn, is "outside" the light, out of which it is formed, and which can "see" the higher meaning.

145. Once we can use the receptive gaze—unmoving attention—we can direct it to the object. When we become identical with it—so that there is no longer any object—we can become aware of the attention that has become the cognitive image of what was the object. Then we can become aware of attention that is not yet imprinted by the "object."

146. The receptive form of perception (in the realm of any sense) is the condition for perceptual meditation. The ability to *produce* receptive perception means that we become aware of the receptive attention, the bridge, as well.

147. After having attained receptive attention in seeing, which is the easiest to work with, we can turn to other senses (hearing, tasting, smelling, touching).

148. Probably the last and most difficult task will be to attain receptive perception in the sense of touch, because touch is the closest to the "me"-feeling, which separates us from immediate and unmediated knowing (See 24).

## Summary and Perspectives

149. When concentration attains a certain intensity, attention begins to flow steadily and effortlessly, and we experience its now restored original nature as joy and healthiness.

150. As attention is in some sense the "substance" of the self, when we concentrate we gather together the dissipated parts of the self.

151. In meditation, emptiness of mind flashes up; and we try to hold it steadily. If we succeed in keeping attention empty, it grows both in intuition and in quality.

152. When attention reaches the stage of identification with the theme in concentration, usually it first has the quality of pure (form-free) thinking/picturing. If we keep it form-free—experiencing it "before" the image—it will change into feeling, and then into receptive willing. "Thy will be done" is the gateway to the idea of the object, that is, to the will that it should function in a certain way.

153. Illusion arises when we do not experience the bridge: when we do not include the bridge in the experience of the "object." When we do not experience the

bridge, duality arises. In the experience of duality, the witness is present only as a shadow. As soon as we experience the bridge, duality ceases.

154. When we start concentrating on a concept and experience the attention of which it is made, any concept is suitable for the letting-go of *all* concepts.

155. Understanding is not-understanding: it stops when *something* is understood.

156. Understand the word "this" and you are in the right place; you need no further instruction.

157. Recognize your attention in every phenomenon—objects, thoughts, feelings, distractions, dreams.

158. There are no phenomena if consciousness does not move.

159. To be unprejudiced means to dissolve concepts, thoughts, and forms, or to let them melt, by concentrating attention so as to attain emptiness. Only the empty mind or consciousness can intuit new ideas. Such emptiness usually happens by chance, in a moment so brief it is not experienced. But if the state of emptiness is experience consciously, it can be used for intuitive research. This presupposes the "I-am"-experience and meditation.

160. This true light penetrates and dissolves everything. Therefore there is nothing to attain—everything is already in it. No seeking, no getting, no grasping, no eliminating.

161. There is no light outside; therefore there is nothing outside. There is no light inside; therefore there is nothing inside. If everything is made of light, where should the border between outside and inside be?

162. We can make mistakes in understanding, but not in experiencing.

163. The general direction is backward: from the object toward the source of attention.

164. Attention ceases to move from point to point, from object to object, when it becomes aware of its own flowing movement: then it stays still. Then the bridge—the awareness of attention being imprinted—begins: the experience that leads attention back to its source from the object.

165. Receptive attention does not move.

166. Strive; make an effort; then relax. If your attention was unmoving, when it relaxes, it will be empty. If it was moving, when it relaxes it will be filled with associations.

167. Attention is formed by the world; attention forms the world.

168. The bridge includes the "I-am"`-experience. In the experience of the bridge, the highest reality is close at hand.

169. Illusion arises when the experience of reality does not include the bridge.

170. As long as we feel ourselves as bodies, our realities will be bodies. As long as we experience ourselves as souls, our realities will be concepts and ideas (formed attention). If we experience ourselves to be spiritual beings, consisting of faculties, our reality will be empty attention or light. The sequence or change in reality begins with perception, turns to concepts and ideas, then to light or empty attention, which conceives the concepts by which we perceive what usually is called reality.

171. Since the "I-am"-experience consists in attention lighting up from within, there is nothing to be attained: everything lights up in this light and absolutely nothing can be attained.

172. What exists and what does not exist is made of empty attention; which therefore neither exists nor does not exist.

173. Since phenomena and Mind are one and the same (as Huang Po says in *The Zen Teachings of Huang Po*, p. 125), the perception of a phenomenon is the perception of Universal Nature: Buddha, Buddha-mind.

174. The light and our perception of it are one.

175. The image consisting of formed attention is seen by the same attention. Such is the miraculous nature of light.

176. To become aware of awareness (or attention) is *being* (not only knowing). This light-filled, communicative

being is love. Or, it is a being that love, if it has lost it, generates anew. It is spaceless and timeless.

177. Love is the force through which we can unite with what is understandable: "I"-beings, ideas, and meanings. Since separation by "me"-feeling occurs in consciousness, union comes about through the same consciousness.

178. Love is light in action in the will. This light is the light of "I"-beings, who, according to their possible changes, are mobile attention and mobile identity, and who are always uncompleted, never finished.

179. Even thinking is beyond subjective and objective; even meaning is timeless and spaceless. Attention does not belong to me, any more than language or thinking do. Therefore, nothing belongs to me.

180. Healing is within us from the beginning.

181. I am always in beginning.

# A Personal Afterword

I HAVE BEEN PRACTICING the exercises described in this book since 1964, when I was forty. I was always experimenting then; and I am still experimenting now. And so I warmly recommend whoever seeks to live a "practicing" life to experiment. Only the most general features of the exercises are describable, yet spiritually we are all highly individual, and this includes how we do the exercises. Everyone must therefore adapt the methods individually, and the best way to do this is by experimenting.

I have experienced various benefits that I attribute to daily meditation practice. By doing exercises, I save time and energy for everyday tasks such as researching, lecturing, doing seminars, and writing.

I do concentration exercises at least once a day. In addition, depending upon the day's schedule, I usually meditate several times. When I am writing, it is almost as if I am meditating continuously—many meditations at a stretch, without a time limit. In fact, it disturbs me when I am working if I know my time is limited—if I know, for instance, that at a certain time I will receive a visitor. My standard daily meditation is the Prologue to the Gospel of St. John.

I have not changed the theme of my concentration exercise since I began in 1964. I use my pair of ivory chopsticks. The inclination to change the theme of concentration usually arises if one's attention is not wholly and one-pointedly concentrated on the theme. This provides an opportunity to compare one's present experience with what one did the day before or a week ago. Then the feeling can arise that one is proceeding in the same way. This might be correct; but if I am wholly concentrated on the theme, there is no place for comparisons.

As a consequence of practicing over many years, I can be fully concentrated if I want to be. Therefore I usually do my meditations without the preceding concentration, which I used to do when I was beginning. Nor, for the most part, do I "reduce" the meditation—for instance, to one word—to reach the unity of the theme (if it is a sentence), as I also used to do for a long time. Similarly the "critical intensity" of attention, which to reach it earlier took at least a few minutes, now usually comes in seconds, after which intensity grows by itself without effort, but with joy—which does not distract me.

# A Meditation

Light (attention) works in identity.

Every object is the result of an identity—which has ceased to be.

Meaning is formed light, free of matter.

We understand what the senses cannot perceive: meaning.

Any content kindles the question: Who experiences it?

Light is form-free.

We are the gift and the recipient of what is given.

Through form to freedom from form.

I am always one with all worlds.

All is now.

Once "tree" also included the experience of the tree.

Only light enters consciousness, which itself is light.

Pure awareness leads to (cognitive) feeling.

We feel only feelings.

Images do not remain in the mirror.

Darkness is experienced by light.

Light is independent of anything that is illuminated by it—that is, it is independent of everything.

The subject is only now.

We cling to what we do not know.

Is this a thought?

Light shines through itself.

The "I-am" is aware of the light.

I can experience thinking, feeling, and willing. And myself.

This is light.

Images arise by seeing.

Thoughts, images: everything vanishes tracelessly into the light.

In the light, there is nothing.

Where there is something, there is someone. And where there is nothing, there is someone.

Every human faculty leads to the self.

Understanding is timeless.

Attention seeks itself.

Light experiences itself in human beings.

Love speaks.

Light is beyond words.

Love is identity and difference, the being of the "I."

The Self has no parts.

If ideas come, we cannot think. If we think, ideas do not come.

The light seeks itself: therefore it shines.

I am the door.

Light is invincible joy.

True attention is love.

True light permeates everything.

The light and our perception of it are one.

Concentrated attention is unmoving.

If light finds itself, its shining multiplies and sings.

Emptiness is the experience of the "I": not this, not that.

The more unmoving, the more cognitive.

# FURTHER READING

(Available from Lindisfarne Books / SteinerBooks—
www. Steinerbooks.org or SteinerBooks PO Box 960
Herndon, VA 20172-0960. Phone (703) 661-1594.
FAX (703) 661-1501)—and through all bookstores)

By Georg Kühlewind:

*Stages of Consciousness: Meditations on the Boundaries
of the Soul.*

*Becoming Aware of the Logos: The Way of St. John the
Evangelist*

*From Normal to Healthy: Paths to the Liberation of
Consciousness*

*The Life of the Soul: Between Subconsciousness and
Supraconsciousnes*

*The Logos-Structure of the World: Language As Model
of Reality*

*Working with Anthroposophy: The Practice of Thinking*

*Star Children: Understanding Children Who Set Us
Special Tasks and Challenge*

*Wilt Thou Be Made Whole? Healings in the Gospels*

By Rudolf Steiner:

*Truth and Science*

*Intuitive Thinking as a Spiritual Path*

*How to Know Higher Worlds*

*Theosophy*

*An Outline of Esoteric Science*

*A Way of Self-Knowledge and The Threshold of the Spiritual World*

By Michael Lipson:

*Stairway of Surprise*

By Massimo Scaligero:

*The Light*

(Available from Rudolf Steiner College Press, 9200 Fair Oaks Blvd., Fair Oaks, CA. Phone (916) 961-8727. Fax (916) 961-8731. www.steinercollege.edu.)

By Georg Kühlewind:

*Schooling of Consciousness: Selected Essays* (Ed. Friedemann Schwarzkopf)

*Thinking of the Heart and Other Essays* (Ed. Friedemann Schwarzkopf)